God Things Come in Small Packages

for FRIENDS

Susan Duke, Judy Carden,
and LeAnn Weiss

To schedule author appearances, write: Author Appearances, Starburst Promotions, P.O. Box 4123, Lancaster, Pennsylvania 17604 or call (717) 293-0939. Website: www.starburstpublishers.com.

CREDITS:
Cover design by Richmond & Williams
Text design by Steve Diggs and Friends, Nashville

All Scripture was taken from the HOLY BIBLE: NEW INTERNA-TIONAL VERSION® NIV®. Copyright© 1973, 1978, 1984 by International Bible Society.

First Printing, October 2000
ISBN: 1-892016-34-6
Library of Congress Catalog Number 00-101267
Printed in USA

Contents

INTRODUCTION

By Susan Duke

My friend shall ever be my friend
and reflect a ray of God to me. —**Thoreau**

$\mathcal{I}$ can't think of a greater example of God's gift of friendship than the story behind the writing of this book. For me (Susan), Judy, and LeAnn, this project is truly a "God Thing." Who would have dreamed that an author in Texas and two in Florida would end up working together?

As I write these words, I have yet to meet one of my beloved writing partners, Judy, face-to-face. Yet, through countless phone conversations, I've come to know the heart of this friend. I'm certain that I could walk into Judy's house (and she in mine), take off my shoes, and be totally myself, because we've established an eternal friendship.

When LeAnn and I met on the last day of a writers conference in 1998, I could not have imagined what God had in store for us! It's not every day that God blesses your life with a friend who unfolds places in your heart you never knew existed, cheers you when you are down, nurtures your dreams, and prays with you.

When friends celebrate life's little pleasures, they are twice blessed. So it's fitting that a tribute of honor be paid to the giver of friendship, the connector of hearts, and our best friend, Jesus. There is no greater friendship or reason to celebrate life than him.

Two are better than one, because they have
good return for their work. —Ecclesiastes 4:9

The Lord has done great things for us, blessing us with the joys of friendship. May God our Father, who loved us and by His amazing grace gave us the gift of eternal comfort and good hope, encourage your heart and strengthen you in every good deed and word.

Psalm 126:3; 2 Thessalonians 2:16–17

TEA FOR TWO

By Susan Duke

Cold and rainy autumn days are perfect for curling up with a good book beside a cozy fire—and that's exactly what I'd planned to do—until the phone rang.

I detected a hint of melancholy in my friend Brenda's voice, as she said, "I was hoping you were home today. I just feel like I need to get away—out of the city for awhile."

"Sure, come on out. I'd love to see you!" I replied. "But are you okay?"

"I guess so. I've had a terribly heavy schedule at work but I'm off this afternoon."

"I'll fix lunch," I said, knowing the forty-five-minute drive from Dallas would give me plenty of time to prepare my famous chicken salad and cheesy soup.

"Please. Don't go to any trouble, Susan. I'm just feeling kind of down and coming to your house cheers me up."

"No trouble. Lunch will be ready when you get here!"

As I scurried about the kitchen, my eyes rested on a silver tea set I'd spontaneously bought a few days before. *Prepare a tea party for Brenda,* a still small voice seemed to whisper. Although I ignored the voice at first, the thought persisted. So, rather than setting the kitchen table, I decided to open the leaves of an Appalachian primitive table that sits by French doors in my family room. I pulled my favorite antique blue-and-white china from the cupboard, gathered my white Battenburg lace placemats and napkins, and put a teakettle of water on the stove. When the kettle whistled, I poured the steaming water over a strainer of Earl Gray tea leaves into the silver teapot. I lit the candles on the table the moment I heard Brenda's knock at my door.

When I led Brenda through the kitchen—and into our transformed "tea room"—she stopped in the doorway and gasped. "Did you do this *just* for me?"

"I certainly did—to let you know how special you are. Besides, we both need a blissful kind of day occasionally, don't you think?"

Surrounded by soft strains of Victorian music, a flickering hearth, and gentle rain falling outside the window, Brenda's gloomy mood quickly changed. As we dined and enjoyed tea for two, I smiled at the thought of how something as simple as a silver teapot turned an ordinary afternoon into a delightful moment to pause and celebrate the blessing of friendship.

It doesn't take a lot of time or money

to show a friend how special they are

to you. Sometimes it's the little things

that create special moments with

blessings for both of you!

$\mathcal{M}$y friend, I thank God every time I remember our times together and the countless ways you've touched my heart. May God bless you and keep you and make His face shine brightly upon you all the days of your life.

Philippians 1:3; Numbers 6:24–26

HANDPRINTS OF TIME

By Judy Carden

Life seemed so simple seventeen years ago on Homekort Avenue—in the days when a silver-haired sweetheart named Selma was my next-door neighbor. On glorious midsummer mornings I'd peer from my kitchen window and watch as she carefully turned the dirt in her garden. She'd wave me over, and we'd talk while she tilled the soil and I bounced a baby on each hip.

That's how our friendship began—a bond forever connected by a decade of brilliant tulip gardens in the spring and snow-covered sidewalks in the winter. The only barrier between our homes was a split-rail fence, a fence my little ones discovered how to navigate through soon after learning their first steps.

Oh, how Selma loved to answer my toddlers' pounding fists on her back porch door, as they came to collect their daily rations of graham crackers. I, of course, was always close behind, rag in hand, ready to wipe the tiny dirt-crusted handprints from her shiny glass door.

"Oh, leave the handprints," Selma would plead with me. "Why, these are precious impressions of love—God's little gifts to me." And so the handprints remained until after the children tumbled back through the slats into their own backyard.

For many years our families co-celebrated birthdays, holidays, holy days, and, of course, there were the "every days" we shared, too—air brushed crimson sunsets from atop the hill on Homekort, the cicada's summer symphonies, autumn's last leaves falling from the old maple tree, and the splendor of a freshly-fallen mantle of snow.

Though time and distance have long since separated our families, Selma's friendship is imprinted in our hearts—in the prayers we pray, the songs we sing, the sunsets we behold, and the people we love. Each time I spy a tiny set of handprints I am reminded of that which I have always known: that our lives were abundantly blessed with love and affection because of a silver-haired sweetheart from the house on Homekort.

How blessed to be the beneficiary of

an intergenerational relationship

often overlooked in today's culture. An

older friend can be our connection to

the past, common sense for the pre-

sent, and coach for the future.

*D*on't settle for mere survival. Come to God when you are tired and stressed out, and He will give you rest. Follow His ways, and He'll show you how to live freely and lightly. May God lead you to abundance and beside quiet peaceful waters. May your heart be refreshed in God.

—————— ● ——————

Matthew 11:28–30; Psalm 23:2; Philemon 1:20

CRYSTAL RIVER RENDEZVOUS

By LeAnn Weiss

$\mathcal{J}$ust past midnight after returning home from the office, I answered a knock at my front door. Perched on my front step, wearing mischievous grins, were my good friends, the Osborne family. "Hey Kookie Lukey, we've missed you," Martha Osborne said as she and three of her grown brothers greeted me with hugs. "We're heading north for a Crystal River rendezvous!"

Having heard many stories of Crystal River getaways and knowing that I would be spending another weekend shuffling through a mountain of paperwork, I replied, "Sounds like fun, but—"

"Good, because you and your sister Pat are coming with us," they said.

After years of managing political campaigns, most of my friends accepted that I was off limits for nonessential socializing during campaign season. I reminded my new friends of my job responsibilities.

"Too bad. Then effective immediately, you are officially kidnapped!" they decreed as they handcuffed me. Despite my good-natured protests, they carried me outside to their van where I was surprised to find Mr. and Mrs. Osborne waiting.

"We're glad you could join us," the couple said.

I thought they were joking. As Martha went back in the house, I explained my predicament to her parents.

Suddenly, Martha reemerged from my house with Pat and our duffel bags. After everyone piled into the van, we sped away.

I expected them to drive around the block and then let me out. Instead, once out of town they took off the handcuffs and informed me that my ransom would be a weekend of fun.

The next morning we awakened at beautiful Crystal River. Pat and I lounged by the Osborne's pool, enjoying our favorite foods. We swam in the river in search of manatees. Later, our hosts towed us behind their boat as we bounced about in inner tubes. Videos, popcorn, and games topped off both nights.

That Monday I returned to the frenzy of campaign life completely refreshed. Today handcuff sightings still evoke chuckles when I recall how friends kidnapped me for a much needed weekend of rest and recreation that I would have missed without their zany intervention.

Friends are often God's agents of refreshment,

relaxation, and no-apology fun on the wild

merry-go-round of life.

Laughter is great medicine for the soul. May we love each other deeply, because love covers a multitude of bloopers and blunders.

———⬤———

Proverbs 17:22; 1 Peter 4:8

THE ROAR OF LAUGHTER

By Susan Duke

$\mathcal{H}$ave you ever had one of those embarrassing moments in the presence of friends that end up marking you for life? My friend Kathy and her husband, Emery, will never let me live down one of those "sacred" moments that occurred when my husband, Harvey, and I were visiting their church.

They have now renamed me Tiger Woman.

It's bad enough that we were seated in the enormous sanctuary's second row, but worse that we were surrounded on all sides by members. When the enthusiastically charged pastor asked the congregation to stand and repeat some of the hearty and valid points he'd be making in his sermon, I jumped right in with the responsive crowd.

"I'm here because I love the Lord!" we all repeated after the dynamic leader.

"And I'm a tither, not a robber!" the pastor continued . . . and we responded again.

Except this time, for whatever reason, my ears didn't hear exactly what the pastor said. In trying to follow the flow of the moment, my mouth spontaneously repeated what my ears "thought" they heard.

"I'm a *tiger*, not a robber!" I exclaimed.

The look on Kathy's face as she turned to me was enough to make us both double over with hysterical laughter. When she finally came up for air and explained to her baffled husband what we were laughing about, the laughter only escalated . . . finally reaching my poor red-faced husband who was trying to remain proper!

It was one of those rare moments when you thank God for friends with whom you can laugh and be silly and miraculously redeem some sense of dignity.

I smile each time I open my e-mail and find a message from Kathy addressed to Tiger Woman. I'm reminded of the joy of friendship when I look at the small stuffed beanie tiger that sits on my computer monitor and the large orange-striped tiger magnet that graces my refrigerator door and growls whenever I press its head. Both are compliments of Kathy and Emery—friends who give me the freedom to *roar* with sacred laughter!

Laughter is good for the soul. When

friends share laughter, even over

mistakes and embarrassing moments,

we unwrap God's gift of freedom

found in genuine friendships.

$\mathcal{M}$ay you go out with joy and be led forth with peace. Be strong and courageous knowing that God is with us wherever we go.

——————————— ———————————

Isaiah 55:12; Joshua 1:9

A FAREWELL TO
REMEMBER

By Judy Carden

$\mathcal{I}$ still remember watching as the moving van, loaded with our family's furnishings, pulled away from the curb in front of my mailbox. I also recall precisely what my heart felt on that blustery autumn afternoon: *Well, here we go again—another move, another set of good-byes.* After a long moment, I turned from the picture window, and feeling very melancholy, walked slowly into my favorite room—my dressing room. Curling up on the carpet beneath the skylight, I whispered my final farewells to the two-story colonial our family called home.

"Knock-knock," echoed my friend Linda's voice from the first-floor entrance foyer. "I'm delivering children. Any takers?"

Wandering past the empty archways of my bedroom suite, I made my way downstairs to what I expected to be a party of six—Linda, her two children, and my three. But as I approached the kitchen, I detected giggling, and then the song, "I Had the Time of My Life" blaring from a boom box. *What in the world is going on,* I wondered. Then I saw them—all of them—my friends and neighbors, gathered in my kitchen, one last time, to give my family a farewell to remember, to turn a typically sad event into an occasion for the sweet celebration of friendship.

"You *really* didn't think we'd let you leave without giving you something to remember us by, did you?" Diana asked.

For hours we harmonized Broadway tunes, laughed, talked, and danced until we were ready to drop. As dusk began to gather outside, our time together drew to an end. I piled the kids into the car to begin our cross-country journey. Teary-eyed friends ran alongside us until we slowly drove from sight. Few displays of affection have touched me as deeply as that one.

It's true; my North Pittsburgh friendships were brief ones, details of everyday events long forgotten. Even though time has erased many of those memories, the picture of our sweet parting is etched in the scrapbook of my mind.

Lord, in those regrettably short

seasons of fellowship, thank you for

thoughtful friends who care enough

to leave us with a thousand

golden memories.

$\mathcal{D}$on't forget all the marvelous benefits of friendship with God. When you're feeling over-whelmed, look up and remember your help comes from the Lord. He forgives us and heals us. When we're feeling low, He redeems us crowning us with His incomparable love and compas-sion. He satisfies our desires with good things and renews our youth like eagles. His law is per-fect, reviving our souls.

Psalm 121:1–2; Psalm 103:2–5; Psalm 19:7

SOARING ON GOD'S WINGS

By LeAnn Weiss

I sure hope no one calls today because I'm fresh out of encouragement, I thought. I considered temporarily changing my business name from Encouragement Company to Discouragement Company. As I tried to write, my mind kept replaying two hurtful situations involving longtime friends that had occurred only days earlier, leaving me emotionally drained. I felt like I'd failed Friendship 101 and wanted to bury my head in the sand like an ostrich.

Hearing the familiar clunk of my mailbox, I went outside to get the mail. *All I need is another stack of junk mail to read.* But as I flipped through the mail, I recognized the graceful penmanship of my dear friend and cross-country writing partner, Susan Duke. *I wonder what Suzie's sent me now?* I thought as I ripped open the small package wrapped in a plain brown paper bag postmarked from Texas.

Inside was a small pewter eagle pin. Suzie's handwritten message in the encouraging card read, "Thank you for nurturing my dreams! Remember, you're an eagle! Here is your first Eagle Medal for soaring on the wings of God's love and inspiration. Your love has given me great joy and encouragement. Happy writing. Happy soaring. Love you, Suzie."

Suzie had also tucked in a calligraphy copy of Isaiah 40:31 that read, "But they that wait upon the Lord shall renew their strength; they shall mount up with wings as eagles; they shall run, and not be weary; and they shall walk, and not faint."

Suzie's timely keepsake gently prompted me to pause for a much needed quiet time with God. After reading my Bible and praying, I once again felt energized and encouraged. My circumstances hadn't changed, but my perspective of life changed as I reexamined my situation from God's panoramic view thanks to the help of my special friend. I taped Suzie's eagle pin and verse to my computer monitor as a daily reminder that waiting on God is my secret to soaring.

Friends help us to soar above

disappointments and storms by

strengthening us with God's Word.

*S*pecial friends stick closer than a brother. God makes us stand firm in Christ. He has anointed us and blessed us with His seal of ownership. He's given His Spirit in our hearts as a deposit, guaranteeing what is to come. May God continue to unite our spirits as we follow Him.

Proverbs 18:24; 2 Corinthians 1:21–22; Romans 15:5

TWINS—SEPARATED AT BIRTH!

By Susan Duke

$\mathcal{W}$hen people tell us how much we are alike, Judy and I often comment, "We're really twins—separated at birth!"

They know we're kidding, but sometimes our similarities are uncanny. We are indeed in the same family; Judy Wood is my niece, born just one month after me. (Becoming an aunt when you're a month old is hard work!) And when you're raised in a blended family, you often have situations like ours where Judy's dad, my much older half brother, and his wife were expecting Judy at the same time my mom was expecting me. So, Judy and I made mud pies as children and grew up sharing a bond beyond family connections, establishing us as lifelong friends.

Ours is that rare kind of friendship that sometimes manifests itself in peculiar ways. Like the time, unbeknownst to me, Judy bought a little framed angel print for me and then secretly decided to keep it for herself. When I drove to my hometown for Thanksgiving and went to Judy's house for an afternoon visit, I walked right up to her antique cupboard door where the little print was hanging and, by pure instinct blurted, "Judy, that's mine!"

Shocked at my spontaneous outburst, Judy confessed immediately. "I know it is! I really bought it for you but liked it so well I kept it. Here," she whined sheepishly, as she gently pulled it from its resting place, "It's yours!"

Even though we live 150 miles apart, we often discover that we've bought the same style, color, and brand of jacket or blouse from the same department store chain. We're always amused when we spot items in our homes identical to something the other of us has recently purchased.

Whether it's laughing at one of the hilarious cards Judy sends, chatting long distance, helping host our family's yearly tea party, or going junkin' (as we call our antique excursions), Judy and I treasure our unique bond. She loves telling people that I'm the oldest . . . by one month. I just tell her that means I'm more mature!

The sweetest thing Judy ever said to me was, "Suzie, you're like my other heart." Judy knows I feel the same way about her. We may not have been birthed as actual twins, but there's no doubt God gave us twin spirits and kindred hearts.

Compatibility goes beyond similar tastes or interests.

A kindred spirit kind of friendship is a deep

understanding and celebration of another's heart.

*C*onsider the great things God has done for us. Remember the history we've made together. Think about our true friendship and the good times we've shared. Reflect on noble things we did, lovely memories, and excellent days. May we continue to fix our eyes on Jesus, the author and perfecter of our faith.

———————— ● ————————

1 Samuel 12:24; Deuteronomy 32:7; Philippians 4:8; Hebrews 12:2

STILL CONNECTED
AFTER ALL THESE YEARS

By Judy Carden

*W*ith a full tank of gas, a backpack stuffed with clothing, and a heart bursting with adventure, I began my journey in Cooperstown, New York. While my husband and sons were entrenched in baseball memorabilia, I embarked on a side trip to visit my best buddy from junior high school days of bobby socks, boys, and braces. It had been years since we had seen each other—twenty-eight to be exact.

For years I had dreamed of the reunion I might someday have with my beloved friend, Carol Profeta. It was as though my restless heart was in search of something that had no name. Some sort of validation, perhaps. So, at long last, on an unseasonably cold July morning, I buckled my seat belt, whispered a prayer for God's blessing, and headed for Fairport.

Making my reentry into the quaint Erie Canal village, my car creaked over the old lift-bridge leading to Carol's house— the very one she and I had crossed hundreds of times as children—and at that moment memories flooded my mind. At last, I hugged Carol. During a whirlwind weekend we reminisced about those innocent times: tender first loves, slumber parties where the boys somehow managed "surprise" appearances, and teachers who impressed us.

Eventually, we moseyed into town to have our picture taken together on the bridge that still whispered tales of our teenage years. We visited former classmates, laughed, cried, and talked some more.

After going nearly nonstop for forty-eight hours, completely covering twenty-eight years, the morning came for me to, once again, bid my friend farewell.

I keep the photograph of us by the lift-bridge on my office desk. Each time I glance at the two of us—arms tightly linked—I am convinced that it is not necessarily the extra-ordinary events that bind hearts through the years. Rather, we become bound to others by our longing to blend the past with the present, knowing that the lives of friends we once loved still matter.

It is those friendships forged from

deep within our hearts that most

tenderly touch our souls. Thank you,

Father, for the gift of "old" friends.

*T*hanks for letting me experience the sweet fragrance of God's love through our friendship. Absolutely nothing, including death, can separate us from His unconditional love. He loves us regardless of our past, present, or future. Even when we are faithless, He remains faithful. His love endures forever and His faithfulness continues through all generations. May God continue to increase the seeds of your life and enlarge your harvest of righteousness.

---

2 Corinthians 2:14; Romans 8:35–39; 2 Timothy 2:13; Psalm 100:5; 2 Corinthians 9:10

MY PERENNIAL GARDEN

By Susan Duke

$\mathcal{M}$oving to the country changed many things in my life, especially the simple methods of city gardening to which I was accustomed. My husband and I discovered that having more ground to tend required massive plantings in the numerous flowerbeds we'd planned.

We soon learned the value of planting perennials—flowers that would faithfully reappear each spring, providing a consistent and harmonious setting for the short-lived but colorful splashes of annuals needing to be replaced each season. Searching for hardy perennials—nature's silent balladeers of steadfast endurance—became an adventure.

One beautiful spring morning as I sat outside planning my gardening chores, my phone rang. "Good morning!" my friend Sonja said. "I'm thinning out my perennials that are coming up all over my garden, and I thought you might like to have some. Pour me a cup of coffee and I'll come on over."

Sonja soon drove into my driveway, opened her trunk, and unloaded armloads of containers brimming with freshly dug Silver King, wild violets, Shasta daisies, coreopsis, and a few other unknown plants. My heart danced with delight at the thought of adding part of my friend's bountiful garden to my own.

A few years later, just before Sonja moved to Kentucky, she brought me a rose bush. "I hope you don't think I'm being egotistical," she laughed. "But the name of this rose bush is Sonja, and I wanted to leave you with something to remember me by!"

Sonja's been gone for several years. Although we are both busy, we keep in contact by phone, eagerly catching up on each other's lives.

I miss Sonja, but year after year I enjoy the sumptuous fragrance and soft peach-tinted blossoms from her rosebush. Every spring, I thin out and share Sonja's Silver King with friends. Every fall I harvest its soft silvery foliage for fashioning herb wreaths.

Just as the imperishable wild violets and yellow daisies appear each summer, God reminds me that perennial friendships are a blessing from him.

Our lives are filled with acquain-

tances who color our world for a time.

But true and enduring friendships

provide an everlasting harvest of

God's blessings that endure through-

out the seasons of our lives.

*G*od hears our prayers. He pulled us from a lonely pit of mud and stood us on a rock giving us firm footing and a new song. When we join together in prayer, God is right there in our midst, no matter how far apart we may be.

——————————— ● ———————————

Psalm 40:1–3; Matthew 18:19–20

ONLY A PRAYER AWAY

By Judy Carden

*O*riginating from different regions of the country, the three of us discovered one another as we sloshed through mounds of mud—each on our own lot—inspecting the freshly poured footers to the basements of our new homes. Though it would be several years before we understood why, something besides the cement took hold that day—between Kay, Linda, and me an inexplicable bond had formed.

Soon after settling into our homes, our families observed fun weekends with backyard barbecues and water balloon fights. We hosted baby showers and exchanged recipes. Perhaps the most meaningful element of our friendship was our unexplainable desire for a deeper prayer life. Naturally, we had no way of knowing how the power of prayer would forever affect our friendship.

Nearly a year to the day after our meeting, I moved out of state. The illness and, ultimately, death of my husband had left my three small children and me reeling. I thought we should live closer to family. But even surrounded by family, I missed Kay and Linda. I felt as if they were still my lifeline, and I clung to them desperately.

And they came through for me when I needed them most.

"Take a piece of construction paper," Kay instructed me one day on the telephone, "and make the first mark of what someday will be a completed circle, representing closure. Each time you feel you have made progress, add to the circle. Meanwhile, Linda and I will be praying for you."

And pray they did, calling the petitions "shooter prayers"— swift, short, urgent prayers, born to help a friend in need. For what seemed an eternity, I struggled and they prayed. But eighteen months later I finally penciled in the mark that completed the circle.

One decade later and twelve hundred miles apart, we still pray for one another regularly. And what, to an unsuspecting eye, may appear to be but a crinkled piece of construction paper with a circle penciled on it is actually God's reminder that the best friends in life truly are *only a prayer away.*

The power of prayer is never diluted by distance.

Dedicate a designated time each day for a worthy

purpose—the state of a friend's heart.

God is your sun and your shield giving you grace and glory. He won't withhold any good thing from you. May God make all grace abound to you. May you experience His sufficiency in all areas of your life so that you will abound in every good work. Don't grow weary in doing good, for in God's perfect timing, you are going to reap a harvest.

——————— ⊛ ———————

Psalm 84:11; 2 Corinthians 9:8; Galatians 6:9

A Perfect Weekend

By Susan Duke

*F*or two years, due to an overloaded speaking schedule and writing deadlines, I'd had to turn down an enchanting invitation from friends for a girl's getaway. This year, despite looming deadlines, I committed myself to going—partly because these friends insisted on working their schedules around mine. "It'll be good for you," they said.

I mentally marked off the days—using the adventure as a reward for finishing a good portion of my writing projects, convincing myself a change of scenery would invigorate my creative juices.

Marla, Brenda, their mom Betty, sister-in-law Faye, and mutual friend Jackie secured hotel reservations in the city, close to shopping, restaurants, and movie theaters. At last, the day arrived. We were like schoolgirls, let out for recess when we met to drive into Dallas. Car and van loaded with overnight bags, snacks, and drinks, we were off for a fun-filled weekend!

In the company of friends you don't have to do anything extravagant to feel like you are celebrating. You're transformed from a responsible, mature woman into a kid ready to leap for joy. And why is it that some friends possess the talent of bringing out the "ham" in you more than others? That's the effect Marla and Brenda have on me. They love to laugh, and their enthusiasm causes my sanguine clown side to emerge! Our times together are energized with giggles and hugs, and affirmations of friendship's blessing.

After some scrumptious Mexican cuisine, we went to our rooms and put on our pajamas. Everyone then congregated in my room, requesting a reading of bedtime stories from the first two, hot-off-the-press *God Things Come in Small Packages* books.

The next morning, after a hearty breakfast, we shopped, ate lunch, and shopped some more. When we said our good-byes, I called my husband from my cell phone, telling him I'd be home soon.

"What did you girls do?" he asked.

"We ate too much, stayed up too late, spent too much money, slept in, and laughed 'till our sides hurt," I said.

"Maybe you should have stayed home," he commented.

"Are you kidding? This is my idea of a perfect weekend!"

We all need friendship getaways

occasionally. They help redefine our

spirits, nurture our enthusiasm for

life, and allow God to renew us with

love and joy.

$\mathcal{T}$hanks for your kindness and compassion. May God reward you for what you have done.

Ephesians 4:32; Ruth 2:12

THE GREATEST GIFT
OF ALL

By Judy Carden

$\mathcal{I}$t was the summer of 1972—the second Friday of my six-week European tour with friends. Feeling rather adventurous as we neared the outskirts of Budapest in our rented Volvo, we stopped in the middle of a dirt road and, with the aid of our English/Hungarian dictionary, enjoyed an hour or so conversing with a group of local farmers.

Afterwards, we drove into Budapest where, without warning, violent stomach spasms began wracking my body. Moments later I passed out. Flagging down a police car, my friends somehow convinced the policeman to escort us to the nearest hospital. Two hours later, with the American Red Cross acting as interpreters, surgeons performed an emergency appendectomy on me.

The next morning when I awakened in St. Stephen's Hospital I was scared, sore, and very homesick. My sense of adventure was depleted. I bit my bottom lip and began to cry. That's when an elderly peasant farmer with a pungent odor, weathered face, and more teeth missing than not began tiptoeing toward my bed. In broken English he said in a loud whisper, "Ah, Miss New York—I love you, I love you!" Then, taking a transistor radio from his shoulder and holding it to my ear, this total stranger consoled me with Louie Armstrong's recording of "Hello Dolly"—Americana style!

Each day for the next week at precisely high noon, the farmer appeared at my bedside with unidentifiable chicken parts, a small chunk of chocolate, and a cup running over with compassion for me, a foreigner and stranger. He treated me as though I were one of his own children.

Though many years have passed, every time I hear Louie Armstrong's "Hello Dolly," my mind's eye still sees the weathered farmer who took the time to make a difference in the life of a frightened foreigner. His friendship fortified my feeble state. This selfless stranger, who had so little, gave so much when he offered me the greatest gift of all—the gift of his friendship.

It takes so little time for a stranger to

become a friend, and friendship, no

matter how fleeting, transcends

barriers of gender, age, and nationality

when we speak the universal

language of love.

$\mathcal{F}$riends are devoted to each other in brotherly love. Thanks for not just being a friend in name only but backing your words of love with acts of kindness.

Romans 12:10; 1 John 3:18

A CUT ABOVE

By LeAnn Weiss

*A*fter a week of torrential rains, the first rays of Florida sunshine peaked through my home office window. *Finally I can write under blue skies again,* I thought, putting on my sunglasses and venturing outside with note pads, laptop, and drink in hand.

Unfortunately, the monsoon weather coupled with two weeks of not being able to mow had transformed my yard into an eyesore. Examining the knee-high grass overgrown with dandelions and a variety of gargantuan weeds, I knew the immediate attention my yard needed would definitely be a chore.

Then I remembered. My new "easy starting" mower was in the repair shop again. A quick phone call revealed my malfunctioning mower would be out of commission for several more weeks.

With another week of rain forecasted, I envisioned my yard growing into an unsightly jungle in our meticulously manicured subdivision. Knowing it couldn't wait another day, I contacted several lawn services, but they were all fully booked.

After several hours of randomly calling yellow pages ads and dozens of attempts at borrowing or renting a lawn mower for the day, I paused to pray. *"Dear God, I hate to bother you about something as small as my grass, but please help! I don't want my yard to reflect a bad image."*

Later that afternoon while writing, I heard the steady whirring of a lawnmower outside my office window. A short time later I went outside hoping to "bribe" whoever was mowing into trimming my lawn too. I was amazed to find my front yard already neatly cut.

Following the engine sounds to the side of my house, I found my dear friend Gloria working up a sweat as she cheerfully battled my lawn. When Gloria heard my SOS on her answering machine, she graciously responded by coming and mowing my yard herself. Knowing I was under a book deadline, she even delivered a delicious steak dinner.

I thank God for friends like Gloria who willingly reach out to meet needs in practical ways immeasurably touching my heart.

Friends are God's hands extended to

help. They find joy, freely going the

extra mile to help a friend in need . . .

just because they care.

*I*n my weak moments, I see God's power perfected and experience His all-sufficient grace. Thanks for loving me at all times and bearing with me even when I'm not at my best. You openly meet needs, practicing hospitality. May God do far beyond all that you can ask or dream according to His power that is working in you.

———————— • ————————

2 Corinthians 12:9; Proverbs 17:17; Romans 12:13;
Ephesians 3:20

LIVE . . . FROM
BOB AND MARY'S!

By Susan Duke

𝒥f you were to ask my neighbors, Bob and Mary, what it's like living next door to me, they'd probably say, "Well, it's not boring—we've learned to expect the unexpected!"

One such unexpected moment came on a frigid November morning in Texas when I was scheduled for a live 7:30 A.M. radio interview by phone. I'd made sure I was up in time to clear my throat of "froggy" morning sounds and was ready—steaming coffee in hand—to follow the faxed instructions received from the Missouri DJ who would be conducting the interview. My notes and the book I'd be discussing were in front of me on my desk. The great thing about doing an early morning radio interview from your home is that you can leisurely sit in your nightshirt while sipping coffee, even on a bad-hair day, and talk to thousands of listeners without anyone ever knowing how you *really* look!

Fifteen minutes before airtime, someone from the station was supposed to call me for a sound check. When the call hadn't come five minutes before the interview time, I picked up my phone's receiver and to my horror discovered there was no dial tone—only silence.

Like an animated video scene on fast forward, I grabbed my glasses, book, notes, phone number of the radio station, and keys. Gown tail flying and teeth chattering, I dove into the car and raced down my long driveway, across the creek, and into Bob and Mary's driveway. I charged into their house (thank goodness the front door was unlocked) like a wild woman and yelled to Mary, "Don't ask any questions; just give me your phone!"

I immediately dialed the radio station, explained the problem, and gave them Mary's number. Mary shook her head in disbelief as she calmly handed me a fresh cup of coffee and I, the barefoot, spike-haired, pajama-clad radio star collapsed into Bob's office chair.

Within seconds, the phone rang. I took a deep breath and answered with as much southern charm as possible. When my thirty minutes of fame were over, I thanked God for friends who are willing to share their phone with a half crazed author and love me just the way I am, never telling the *real* behind-the-scene story of being live . . . on the air!

When you find a friend with whom you can be yourself,

even on your worst days, you've found a friend who

accepts your weaknesses as well as your strengths and

loves you anyway.

We are able to love because God first loved us. May the Lord make our love increase and overflow for each other. May He direct our hearts into God's love and Christ's perseverance. Surely His goodness and mercy will follow us all the days of our lives and we will dwell in His house forever.

——————— ✳ ———————

1 John 4:19; 1 Thessalonians 3:12; 2 Thessalonians 3:5

I SECOND THAT DEVOTION

By Judy Carden

$\mathcal{N}$estled next to my husband on a cold winter's night I can tell by his steady breathing pattern that he is nearly asleep. After all, it's already eleven thirty—well past our usual bedtime. Earlier this evening, Bob surprised the four of us—my three children and I—with dinner at our favorite restaurant to celebrate the tenth anniversary of his adopting the children. But I'm a long way from slumber. I have a collection of questions clogging my brain. "Hey, Bob," I whisper, tugging at his T-shirt. "Are you awake?"

"I am now. What's up?"

"What would you have done if I had had five children when we met?"

"Married you. Can I sleep now?" he asks groggily.

"How about ten children?" I tug again. "And be honest."

"I'd still have married you. Can I sleep now?" he asks in mock exasperation, but even in the darkness I can tell he is smiling.

Not that I have ever questioned his love for me. Or his commitment. Even in the beginning. When I was able to look past his chiseled good looks, it was his kindness, faithfulness, and unwavering devotion—all qualities that one looks for in a friend—that taught me the true meaning of love.

Bob's right. Had I had ten children when we met, I believe he still would have embraced the opportunity of having ten children to love, ten children to call his own. That's just the kind of man he is.

For a moment, my mind's eye carries me back to our earlier celebration—to the look of love on my husband's face as he listens to his family's incessant chattering. Then, from beneath the blankets, the sound of Bob's steady breathing breaks my spell. But this time I do not disturb his slumber. Instead, leaning into him, I plant a gentle kiss on his shoulder. Placing my head back on the pillow, I know that I have just kissed my very best friend goodnight.

Blessed is the woman who recog-

nizes that, sometimes, she need look

no farther than the man she married

to find her very best friend, for love

and devotion are often only a

heartbeat away.

*T*aste and experience God's absolute goodness. He satisfies the thirsty and fills the hungry with marvelous things. It's my prayer that the eyes of your heart would be enlightened, that you would know the hope to which He called you, the riches of His inheritance, and His incomparably great power for those of us who believe.

——————— · ———————

Psalms 34:8; 107:9; Ephesians 1:18–19

A SWEET REMINDER

By LeAnn Weiss

"Think of your favorite food," my friend Joe said during a time of sharing at my church December 1, 1996.

Without hesitation, I pictured an ice cream sundae covered with whipped cream, chocolate, nuts, and a cherry . . . and got a sudden urge to head straight toward the nearest Baskin Robbins.

"Now think of a friend you've been praying for over an extended period who isn't a Christian yet," Joe continued.

Out of my many unsaved friends, Austin* came to mind as it was his birthday and I had prayed a special blessing for him earlier that morning. Austin has earned my respect by consistently demonstrating integrity, fairness, dependability, compassion, and unwavering character. If heaven's admission were earned by good works, Austin would be near the front. Although he's tolerant of others' beliefs, Austin doesn't believe in God.

Joe shared how his friend had given up coffee for six months and prayed for Joe's salvation. Joe challenged us to consider

* Name has been changed.

fasting from our favorite food. "If you feel God is leading you to do this, each time you want to eat that food, pray for your friend instead."

With my love of ice cream, Austin quickly became among the most consistently prayed for people on the planet. All my family and friends knew that ice cream ranked as the most essential food in my unorthodox "diet," so they were shocked to see me turning down milk shakes, ice cream cones, and my nightly heaping bowl of ice cream. As I explained my ice cream fast, no one really took it seriously at first. My family even forgot and ordered my traditional ice cream birthday cake.

Surviving four years without ice cream, I have surpassed even my own expectations. I know giving up ice cream won't force my friend Austin or others I'm praying for to become Christians. While God desires friendship with each of us, he won't violate our wills. Each ice cream cone or carton of Ben & Jerry's I forgo is a sweet reminder of my commitment to pray that my friends will enter into a personal relationship with God and become my friends forever.

Every taste of joy we experience in

our earthly relationships is merely a

delicious foretaste of what God has

waiting in heaven. A shared love of

God establishes friendships forever.

Where the Spirit of the Lord is, there is freedom. The law of the Spirit of life in Jesus has set us free to experience His abundant life. May God fill us with joy in His presence and with eternal pleasures at His right hand.

_____ ❈ _____

2 Corinthians 3:17; Romans 8:2; John 10:10; Psalm 16:11

TIME TO PLAY

By Susan Duke

"*H*i, this is Charlet. I was wondering if you could come out and play today?"

I could hardly believe my forty-something-year-old friend's gleeful tone of voice when I answered the phone. It made me giggle and instantly answer, "Of course, I'd love to!"

"Then I'll be over around ten o'clock this morning, and we'll have a girl's day out."

I usually was the one to make spontaneous plans, but this time my normally quiet natured and soft-spoken friend Charlet took the lead. I was delighted at the bold invitation and smiled as I thought of how much Charlet had changed in the past year.

Although still mild mannered, she was no longer the shy, reserved woman I'd first known—before I introduced her to Aretha Franklin and the wonderful effects her music can have on house cleaning motivation (a new revelation for Charlet as a pastor's wife!). This was before we discussed why it's okay to be childlike in our faith and relationships.

Of course we must be mature adults, but it's nice having friends with whom you can be a kid at heart, assured that they understand the difference between being childish and childlike.

When Charlet arrived, she handed me a package. "This is something I found that reminded me of our friendship and what it has meant in my life," she said.

Inside the box was a picture of two little girls who were holding bears and having tea. Before I could comment, Charlet explained, "This picture represents how you've brought out the little girl in me that was always hiding in my heart. And this is the kind of friends we will always be, no matter how old we get."

I hugged the gold-framed treasure to my heart. "I will cherish this always," were the only words I could mutter.

No more words were needed. We hugged, brushed away sweet tears, and went out to play.

In the midst of all of our adult respon-

sibilities, it's refreshing to give our-

selves permission every once in

awhile to remember the kid that still

lives within our hearts. Those times

allow our soul to play and joyfully

and spontaneously celebrate the

freedom of friendship.

*T*hanks for the love our friendship brings to me. I pray that God would strengthen you with power through His Spirit in your inner being. Christ dwells in your heart through faith. May you catch a glimpse of God's indescribable love for you that even surpasses the most delightful expressions of human love. May your life overflow with the fullness of God.

——————— ⬤ ———————

Ephesians 3:16–19

A LITTLE LOVE
GOES A LONG WAY

By Judy Carden

$\mathcal{W}$edged in between cardboard moving boxes, I stared blankly at the living room walls, wondering if I could ever *really* be happy living back in Winter Haven. In my twelve-year absence, I discovered, after returning "home," that most of my old friends had married and moved on. My life felt as empty as the walls that surrounded me.

One afternoon, having just returned from the store, I spotted a plate of goodies on my front doorstep. Relieved that our four-legged friend from next door hadn't discovered it, I picked up the blue plastic plate full of fudge walnut brownies covered in clear wrap. Attached was a note from my real estate agent's wife: "I'm so happy that you and your precious children have found a home here in Winter Haven. I just know our friend-ship will be a special one. Love, Susan Dantzler."

After I granted a rare dispensation allowing us to enjoy dessert before dinner, the children and I devoured the entire plate of brownies with a half-gallon of ice-cold milk. To be sure, Susan's hospitality helped us to feel welcome and wanted.

That evening when phoning to thank her, I discovered that Susan and I shared many common interests, not the least being that neither of us had ever met an ounce of chocolate we didn't like!

It wasn't long before the plate began to crack and chip, but each time I started to toss it in the trash thoughts of my friend's hospitality stopped me.

It has been eleven years since Susan placed the plate of brownies on my front doorstep, and our friendship has proved to be an endearing one. The blue plate, however, also holds a special place in my home and heart. It is the keepsake that reminds me to bake that batch of brownies or cookies for someone in need—to take the time to make friends feel loved and wanted. It's the little things that often mean the most. Susan's fudge walnut brownies are the sweetest proof that a little love goes a long way.

We never know just where the bonds of friendship will

take us, but we can be sure that a plate of homemade

TLC is the sweetest place to start.

Your love has lifted my heart.

Thanks for cheering me on to

love and good deeds by encour-

aging and building me up.

Hebrews 10:24; 1 Thessalonians 5:11

LET'S DO LUNCH

By LeAnn Weiss

$\mathcal{N}$orma cornered me at church. "LeAnn, you're too busy. You've been on our hearts for months, and we need to set a firm lunch date." Since our lunch plans had been postponed several times, she opened my appointment book, selected a date, and wrote, "Lunch with Norma and Debbie. No cancellations accepted!"

When the day of our luncheon arrived, we walked between the tables in the restaurant, pausing to say hello to our friends the Wallochs and Terri Irvin, who were eating in one corner. I noticed several long tables had been pushed together. "Let's sit over here," Norma instructed as she seated me at the end of that table. I should have guessed something was up, but I didn't.

Soon dozens of church friends joined us. It wasn't my birthday, and I couldn't think of any special occasions. *There must be a church leadership meeting today and Norma and Debbie were too embarrassed to cancel after insisting I attend,* I reasoned.

Despite the laughter of friends at the other end of the table, I didn't get suspicious until my pastor's family showed up and asked if they could sit next to us. He had cut our church service short that morning because he wasn't feeling well.

Norma stood up and quieted the room. "LeAnn, we know you're puzzled. We are here today to celebrate your friendship and the many ways your encouragement has blessed each of us over the years."

After they prevented me from crawling under the table, my pastor led a series of euphoric ice tea and coke toasts. Debbie presented me with a basket of small gifts and thank you cards, including many from church friends who couldn't attend.

Only a handful of people knew I was planning a trip to Africa for my parents' twenty-fifth anniversary and my sister's graduation. So I was shocked when Norma handed me an envelope with a gift of almost five hundred dollars from my friends for my trip.

I returned from lunch not only full from the savory Italian cooking but also lifted from the generous love and encouragement of dear friends.

Friends create special occasions to

celebrate friendship. They encourage

and build each other up daily,

cheering one another on to love

and good deeds.

*I*n God's loving hands is the life of every creature and the breaths of our lives. The Lord is loving to all He has made and righteous in every way. He created all things and holds our very being. A righteous person cares for the needs of his animals.

Job 12:10; Psalm 154:17; Revelation 4:11; Proverbs 12:10

FOR THE LOVE OF FUR
FRIENDS

By Susan Duke

*W*hen coyotes attacked our black schnauzer, Remus, an abandoned dog we'd recently rescued, we were advised by a veterinarian to have him put to sleep.

We couldn't do it.

Instead, we found a veterinarian who agreed to treat him at her office. After three days, she called to alert us that Remus' condition didn't seem to be improving. "He's still critical, and I'm even more concerned about him now because he's so depressed."

Although we hadn't given much thought to a dog being depressed, we left immediately to visit our wounded friend.

My heart warmed at the tenderness my husband, Harvey, portrayed as he stroked and talked to Remus, reassuring him he'd soon be back home in his warm bed. The slow wagging of his little tail and the look in his liquid brown eyes told us he believed every word. After that first visit and subsequent visits for the next few days, Remus made a turn toward a complete, joyful, and healthy recovery.

With our busy schedules, there are times Harvey and I are tempted to agree with some who've suggested that caring for Remus, Heidi, and our feline companions—Miss Lilly, Scruffy, Mr. Gray, and Cow-cat—is too much trouble. But our hearts know the truth. Their gift of unconditional love far outweighs any inconvenience of including them in our lives.

Even our surprise woodland visitor, a mama raccoon we've named Ramona, comes nightly to our back door (often with her three babies) for her ration of cat food and water. Now that we've earned her trust, she allows us to sit close by while she confidently stretches, poses for snapshots, and occasionally eats from our hand.

I often wonder if we humans place enough merit on our furry friends' emotions—the love they crave and so willingly bestow. Life might be easier without the extra responsibilities of tending to our fur friends. But on cold wintry nights while snuggled beside a warm fire or on moonlit summer evenings as soft southern breezes blow against our faces, we are blessed by sharing life's simple pleasures with friends who faithfully fill our hearts with their unconditional love.

God created every living thing for a

purpose. Through all of his creation,

he sends special blessings—small

tokens of his love, grace, and wonder

into our lives.

*B*ecause the Lord is our light, our salvation, and our stronghold, we don't need to fear. Remember, we are God's workmanship, created in Him to do the good works He's already prepared us for. May we stand firm in one spirit, contending as one, without being frightened by opposition or obstacles. May we serve together with the strength of the Lord.

——————————— ◦ ———————————

Psalm 27:1; Ephesians 2:10; Philippians 1:27–28;
1 Peter 4:11

THE FEARSOME FOURSOME

By Judy Carden

*W*ith graduation only days away, I was determined to fill the remaining scrapbook pages with the dozen or so newspaper clippings that highlighted Aubrey's high school achievements. After a morning of cutting and pasting, I slapped the book shut. Standing to stretch, I accidentally stumbled over a well-worn notebook on the floor.

I read the words inked on its cover: "The Fearsome Foursome's Secrets to Sanity—Do Not Lose!" *Ah,* my heart warmed. *The notebook.*

Picking up the notebook, I eased into my favorite chair and mentally retraced how the Fearsome Foursome had formed two years earlier when our children were elected as junior class officers. Of course, we moms were seasoned enough to know the truth: Kids win elections; parents do the work. Not surprisingly, there wasn't a line of parents waiting in the wings to volunteer for the toughest task on campus: chairing the final two years of fund-raisers for Winter Haven High School's class of 1998. Consequently, Kim, Karen, Lynn, and I accepted the task by default.

Thumbing through the notebook, I was carried back to rainy day flea markets in muddy fields, food fights, and fist-fights. "Mind over matter" became our motto during Monday Prom Committee meetings. Through it all though, the Fearsome Foursome remained in one accord. Hunched over many a McDonald's lunch table, notebooks in hand, we discussed not only our fundraising efforts, but also our hopes and dreams for our children. We swapped both funny and not-so-funny stories. When one of us fell short on energy, the others graciously picked up the slack. And, above all, we prayed.

Nearly two years have passed since our group disbanded, yet what I most fondly recollect is that we four moms had as much fun as—if not more than—the kids did.

The sound of footsteps jarred me from my daydream. I placed the old notebook in its spot on the bookshelf. And I smiled, remembering how the Fearsome Foursome sought nothing more than survival during our "term" and found friendship along the way.

God is so good—for he bathes us in

his blessings when he transforms

friendship fashioned from teamwork

into a timeless treasure of memories.

The unfolding of God's Word gives light and generates hope. Even when our spirits are faint and we think we've lost our way, God knows the perfect path for each of us. May God instruct you and teach you in the way you should go. May He counsel you and watch over you.

——————— ◦ ———————

Psalm 119:130; Romans 15:4; Psalm 142:3; Psalm 32:8

PRACTICING WHAT I
PREACH

By LeAnn Weiss

$\mathcal{I}$ was surprised when one of my personalized bookmarks dropped out from the envelope I opened from Carole Murphy, one of my new customers. For years, I've customarily tucked a little personalized gift in with each Encouragement Company order to brighten the recipient's day.

Carole's note opened with a thank you for the extras I had included with her order. I skimmed the four-page letter, looking for an explanation for the returned bookmark.

When Carole and I had talked earlier, it was obvious she shared my passion for encouraging others and I had asked for her feedback.

Following several pages of constructive suggestions, Carole wrote, "I hope I have not overstepped my bounds in being so honest, but I felt I had to share what was on my heart." Committing to pray for me, she continued, "I am sending this Proverbs 3:5–6 bookmark back to you because it is your verse for today. I pray that I have not offended you in any way."

I picked up the bookmark and read, "Trust in Me with All of your heart! DON'T rely on your own limited understanding. Acknowledge Me, in ALL you say and do . . . and I promise I will guide you. Love Always, Your Awesome God. P.S. Remember, I have the advantage of seeing the entire picture and the end product."

The returned bookmark couldn't have been more timely. After days of weighing the pros and cons of a life-changing decision, I was still engulfed in confusion. By reading the familiar words on the bookmark, I realized I wasn't living what I had written. As I prayed, "Father, forgive me for not trusting you with this decision; please show me the way to go," peace flooded my heart. I knew I could trust God with the outcome.

Weeks later, Carole and I met for the first time when she accompanied me on an out-of-state trip. I thanked her, saying that God had sent her to me as a friend who was sensitive, yet bold enough to speak God's words of truth I needed to hear.

Sometimes when we overlook the obvious, God taps us

on the shoulder through the boldness of friends who

speak the truth in love.

Love is the greatest gift. May we love one another as God loves us. He loves us with an everlasting love and draws us to him with loving-kindness.

1 Corinthians 13:13; John 15:12; Jeremiah 31:3

PATCHES OF LOVE

By Susan Duke

$\mathcal{I}$t never fails. Whenever I look at my red, white, tan, and green antique quilt hanging across an old cupboard door, I think of my friend Sue—probably because of the countless hours she put into restoring its deteriorated tan fabric.

The moment I spotted the old patchwork beauty on a quilt-show bargain table, I admired its rare pattern, color combination, and near perfect tiny stitches. I'm certain the bargain price was because of its obvious flaws—a wide tattered border and pieces of badly deteriorated fabric throughout the quilt. But I knew, with a little expert handiwork, the quilt was large enough for the border to be cut away and the frayed fabric pieces to be replaced without disturbing the overall beauty of the masterpiece.

There was only one problem. I have zero sewing skills. So, I called Sue—who loves old quilts as much as I do. Since she'd recently enrolled in quilting classes, I thought she might recommend someone to do the work. I was pleasantly surprised when she volunteered to tackle the job herself. "I'd love to work on your beautiful quilt," she said. "It will give me experience for future quilt restorations."

I was delighted at the thought that Sue's careful stitching would be interwoven with the remnants of an unknown woman's life. I love pondering about the woman who transformed tiny pieces of fabric from scraps of clothing and created what is treasured today as a work of art: *Did she meet weekly with friends to sew and fellowship? Did she work on her quilt by the light of glowing hearth embers after her household was quiet and chores done? Or did she pray as she painstakingly and patiently saw her project to completion?*

I'll never know the woman who created my beautiful patchwork treasure. But I love imagining that the beauty and excellence of the quilt is the reflection of this woman's legacy. Part of that legacy lives on in the restoration I see lovingly stitched over one hundred years later—reminding me of my special friend Sue, who has sewn much love into the fabric of my life.

Our lives are like patchwork quilts.

And God, the Master Quilter, pieces

together a legacy of friendships that

will warm our hearts for eternity.

Children are a gift from the Lord. God has ordained praise from the lips of children. When we welcome a child in Jesus' name, we're welcoming Him.

Psalm 127:3; Psalm 8:2; Matthew 18:5

TREASURES FROM T. J.

By Judy Carden

After the empty moving van pulled away from the house across the street, I took a head count. *One, two, three, and baby makes four children. Wow, will they breathe life back into this old neighborhood!* I thought, watching with amusement as the little ones, whose parents we knew but hadn't seen in some years, tumbled about in their front yard.

Several days later I heard a tap on the front door. Five-year-old T. J. Brown, a darling Dennis the Menace duplicate, complete with the unruly tuft of yellow hair, awaited me. Keeping his hands locked tightly behind his back, he stood there fidgeting for a long moment. "Here! These are for you," he announced, thrusting a loosely bound bouquet of red roses into my arms.

"Why T. J.," I exclaimed, "they're beautiful! Thank you, little buddy."

"Put them in water," he reminded me, and with one quick twist, the little rascal raced back across the street while his family peered from their front picture window. Thus, our friendship began.

Though I'm inclined to think that T. J.'s gift of roses had more to do with his wanting to hang out with my teenage sons who sport ball uniforms and travel about town in a shiny red truck, he was also probably responding to the kid-friendly, everybody's-welcome atmosphere of our home.

The slap of T. J.'s tennis shoes echoes through our house these days. Serving as a good-time ambassador, he transports treasures—anything from fresh baked goods, courtesy of his mother and sisters, to creepy crawlers, courtesy of T. J.—from their house to ours. It's a foot race to the front door when I spot his face peeking through the glass, for his sense of adventure inevitably resuscitates my spirit.

Each time the little rascal bounces about our family room, I relive the wonder of life through the eyes of a child. T. J.'s capacity to transform a ho-hum moment into a razzle-dazzle rendezvous is the very element of friendship my own forty-something heart had been in search of.

Children are God's greatest good-time

ambassadors. They're able to make a

friend and be a friend by simply

taking everyday moments and teaching

us how to tuck them into our hearts as

keepsake treasures.

*A*lone, we can be overpowered. But a three-cord friendship with God at the center is not easily broken. God knows the plans He has for us. Plans to prosper us and not to harm us. He has a hope and future destined for each of us. When we call upon Him, He listens. Be confident that God will complete the good work He has started in us.

———————— ⬩ ————————

Ecclesiastes 4:12; Jeremiah 29:11–14; Philippians 1:6

THE COVENANT RING

By Susan Duke

"*W*here's your ring?" Jo gasped, staring at the empty place on Janice's index finger.

"I gave it away," Janice explained. "I know it's one of a kind, but my friend Patsy was so intrigued by it, I felt that God wanted me to give it to her. I told her it would be a symbol of our friendship and a reminder of our covenant to pray for each other."

Knowing the sentiment the ring held for Janice and that it had been cast by Janice's father-in-law, who was a jeweler, Jo secretly commissioned the identical casting of another one. When the unique ring, featuring a plain gold cross centered inside the Christian fish symbol, was finished, Jo presented it to Janice as a token of their own special friendship.

Several years later, Janice attended a gathering where I was speaking and our friendship was born. When I returned to the area to speak a few months later, Janice introduced me to her friend Joanna and then invited me to speak for her yearly retreat. During that retreat, I met another of Janice's close friends—Brenda. They took me under their wings and loved me into their friendship circle, a circle that continues to grow eight years later.

The first Christmas after we met, Janice had some of her old gold rings melted down and made into new fish rings. She presented me, Brenda, and Joanna with a gift we will always cherish—our covenant friendship rings.

Whenever I wear my ring, I feel my friends' love and prayers. I also enjoy sharing its story when others admire and inquire about its significance.

Even more valuable than the beautiful fourteen-karat gold ring that rests on my index finger is what it represents—the priceless gift of covenant friends—friends united by God and bound together with golden strands of prayer and heavenly friendship.

When we join in prayer, we receive a

double blessing as friends. We not

only unite in the corporate power of

prayer, but also gain the power of

trusting a beloved friend

with our hearts.

$\mathcal{M}$ay God's love and truth always protect our friendship. Earnest counsel is a pleasant benefit of transparent friends. May we know God's freeing truth. I pray that our love will flourish in knowledge and depth of insight, so that we may be able to discern God's best and may be pure and blameless until the day of Christ.

———————— ● ————————

2 John 1:3; Proverbs 27:9; John 8:32;
Philippians 1:9–10

TENDER TRUTHS

By Judy Carden

$\mathcal{R}$eaching for a tissue for the umpteenth time, I blew my nose, folded it, and tossed it into the pile of soggy squares.

"He is so short-sighted and stubborn and I am, I am, so . . . right," I wailed to the four walls after Bob's and my first major misunderstanding. We were two months shy of our one-year anniversary.

Perhaps I've married the wrong man, I thought. That made me cry so hard I was able to ignore the sudden *brring* of the telephone. Irritated by its continuing noise, however, I gave in and answered it. And oh, how I wished I hadn't. On the other end was my friend Millie—certainly the holiest woman I had ever met. I couldn't bear for her to sense the dire state I was in, so I pretended I was fine. *Certainly she has never felt like I do.*

My false bravado was a fiasco, for my friend sensed my sadness. "What's wrong?" Millie gently pressed.

I proceeded to tell her.

After what seemed an eternity, Millie broke the silence. "Why Judy," she began, her sweet southern drawl immediately soothing my soul. "May I share something with you?"

I nodded my head "yes"—as though she could actually see me.

Millie revealed a closely guarded secret: "Years ago, when Frank and I were newlyweds, we also had a disagreement that wouldn't go away. I felt just as you do now. In fact," she continued, "I remember one evening when Frank pulled the car into the driveway, I thought, *I wish he'd pull into someone else's driveway today*. That was thirty years ago," she said, breaking into a fit of laughter. "So believe me—with patience, prayer, and a great sense of humor—everything will work out."

Millie was right. The timely counsel of a wise friend made me happy to hear Bob's Blazer as it rolled into its rightful place in our driveway.

When truth and transparency become basic tenets of a

relationship, the very "humanness" of those actions may

well be a horizon of hope to a friend's heavy heart.

*F*riends carry each other's burdens. Thanks for thinking of my interests and imitating God by living a life of love, just as Christ loved us and gave Himself up for us as a fragrant offering and sacrifice to God. We can't demonstrate a greater love than laying down our lives for our friends.

———————————— ⬤ ————————————

Galatians 6:2; Philippians 2:4; Ephesians 5:1–2;
1 John 3:16; John 15:13

THE GIFT OF LIFE

By LeAnn Weiss

$\mathcal{F}$or over ten years doctors had monitored Linda's health because kidney disease ran in her family. Still Linda was shocked to discover during an annual checkup that her kidneys were suddenly failing. Family members could not donate a kidney. Linda's youngest sister had already donated a kidney for their mom's transplant, her other sister had undergone a kidney transplant herself, and her brothers had high blood pressure.

Facing confining dialysis without a kidney transplant, Linda returned to Bethlehem Baptist Christian Academy where she taught second grade. She shared her burden with her fellow staff members, requesting prayer.

One day her friend and fellow teacher, Debbie Thorpe, stopped her. "Linda, I'm curious. What's the first step someone would take if they were considering becoming a donor?" she asked.

"The person would have to have the same blood type as the recipient," Linda explained.

Without telling Linda, Debbie had her blood tested and found out that she had the same blood type.

After much prayer, Debbie talked to Linda about the next step and was tested for compatibility. To everyone's amazement, they matched. On March 23, 1999, Debbie underwent surgery to donate one of her kidneys to her friend.

Linda and Debbie had prayed that they would be able to be roommates. Normally hospital policy frowns upon this, but the only available beds on the floor were side by side, enabling the two friends to talk and pray together until they were released four days later.

Although Debbie had complications, she returned to her kindergarten class after six pain-filled weeks of bed rest. She was thrilled when Linda returned to teaching the next fall.

Linda knows Debbie's selfless act of friendship gave her a second chance at a life free from the dialysis. Out of the 3,712 kidney transplants with living donors, only 153 did not involve a relative or a spouse. When Linda thinks of Debbie's gift, she's reminded of Christ. "Just like I can never repay Debbie for my kidney, I can never thank God enough for the priceless gift of Jesus at Calvary."

Friends are often heroes, coming to

our rescue despite inconvenience,

cost, or suffering to share our

burdens. There is no sacrifice

too big for a true friend.

We are no longer foreigners, but fellow citizens with God's people and members of God's household. Good news from a distant land is refreshing to a weary soul. When we seek the Lord, we lack no good thing. His divine power has given us everything we need for life and godliness through our knowledge of Him. We can't even begin to imagine all of the awesome things God has prepared for those of us who are His friends.

——————— • ———————

Ephesians 2:19; Proverbs 25:25; 2 Peter 1:3;
Psalm 34:10; 1 Corinthians 2:9

NO DISTANCE TOO FAR

By Susan Duke

*T*he unusual postmark on the envelope caught my eye. *Who could be writing me from West Nigeria, Africa?*

I was surprised to find a four-page letter and photograph from a young African man whom I'd never met. His name was Daniel. I had no idea how he had gotten my name or heard of my ministry. The letter was a well-written testimony of what being a Christian meant to Daniel and also included a detailed description of his family.

Daniel revealed that he'd gotten my name from a radio broadcast he'd heard a few years before. I had been the guest soloist for a national evangelist who regularly sent tapes to fourteen countries in Africa. Although I'd always dreamed of going to Africa, I counted it a blessing to reach out via tapes. You never know in these situations if anything you say or do impacts or touches lives. But when Daniel's letter came, God reminded me that nothing we do for others is wasted.

The letter Daniel wrote was an unexpected blessing and confirmation that we serve an awesome God who is able to reach across continents to touch a life. My tears flowed as I read Daniel's simple request. "Please, Miss Susan, help me learn more about my God. If you have music or teaching tapes, I would be blessed to receive any help you can send. I only want more of him in my heart. You touched my life through your music, and now you are my beloved friend. Respectfully, your friend forever, Daniel."

I wrote to my new friend, Daniel, and sent him my first book and some tapes and articles. When I took the package to the post office, the postmaster noticed the unusual address. "Africa!" he said. "This will cost you quite a bit to send all that way. You must have family or a very special friend there."

"As a matter of fact, I do," I smiled.

I may never meet Daniel, but we continue to pray for one another through letters, knowing that despite distance, God has given us a unique gift of friendship.

God can connect hearts that may

never meet face-to-face. He can reach

beyond race, religion, and oceans to

create a bond of friendship that

speaks a universal language

of its own.

Your love has given me great joy and encouragement, refreshing my heart. Remember every good and perfect gift is from God. His way is perfect. May He restore your soul and guide you in paths of righteousness. May you be satisfied with God's bountiful provisions.

―――――――― ⬤ ――――――――

Philemon 1:7; James 1:17; Psalms 18:30; 23:3; Jeremiah 31:14

MOUNTAIN MEMORIES

By LeAnn Weiss

$\mathcal{A}$ugust third, instead of celebrating with friends, Jeanenne uneventfully ushered in her dreaded fortieth birthday while traveling home to Orlando after a family camping trip. She tried to hide her disappointment when her husband, Terry, told her that his plans for her birthday had been postponed.

Weeks later, Terry finally revealed that her birthday surprise would be a special November visit from her best friend, Diane, who had moved to Washington State two years earlier.

At last November came. On the way to the airport to pick up Diane, Terry handed Jeanenne a small belated birthday gift. She unwrapped a palm-sized book titled *Afternoon Tea: Making Memories with Friends*, a journal, stationery, and pens.

"I thought you could use these," Terry explained. "I've made special arrangements for you and Diane to fly to North Carolina tomorrow. A rental car will be waiting for your drive to the mountain cabin I've reserved."

"I can't believe you'd do this. What about the kids?" Jeanenne asked.

"Don't worry, I've taken care of all the details. I just want you to enjoy time away with your friend."

Jeanenne was overwhelmed by her husband's creativity and thoughtfulness.

The next morning, Jeanenne and Diane departed for their unexpected getaway to a spacious mountain home. For five days they awoke to a breathtaking view of the sparkling lake below, hiked through the woods, laughed, watched sappy videos together, and enjoyed spontaneous fun without husbands, children, or interruptions. Sipping tea together by the fireplace, they read the book from Jeanenne's husband and wrote insights gleaned from each other.

Refreshed from the mountain experience, Jeanenne couldn't wait to share all of the details with her generous husband who had made it possible. She knew that Terry's incredible gift of time alone with her friend had created memories that would last a lifetime . . . and was well worth the wait.

Knowing women's hearts speak the

same language, one of the greatest

ways that a loving husband can build

intimacy in his friendship with his

wife is to grant her the freedom to

spend quality time with girlfriends.

May the Lord answer in your distress. May He send you help from heaven and grant you support. May He give you the desire of your heart. We will shout for joy when you are victorious. Remember, the Lord saves His anointed and answers from heaven with the saving power of His right hand. Many people place their security in all the wrong places, but we will trust in our 100 percent faithful God. Even when we don't know what to pray, Jesus is at the right hand throne of God interceding for us.

———————— ◦ ————————

Psalm 20:1–8; Romans 8:26

PLINK!

YOU'VE GOT PRAYERS

By Judy Carden

$\mathcal{W}$e had just received the results of Ryan's CT scan, ordered to identify an abnormal mass growing in his chest wall. Test results detected a spot on his liver as well. His blood count was also abnormally low. The next step was to meet with doctors at All Children's Hospital in St. Petersburg to discuss impending surgery. Overcome with grief, I cried until I could cry no more.

Some time later I shut myself in my home office, e-mailing loved ones to ask for prayer for Ryan. Shortly, though, my devastation returned, and I slumped to the floor unable to pray even the simplest prayer. It was the darkest day of my life.

I barely heard the *plink* sound from my computer, indicating that I had incoming e-mail, and I wasn't even sure I cared. But others cared for me. Though *I* was temporarily incapable of prayer, family friends Henry and Marcy Philpot were not.

In part, this is what their e-mail said, "You need to be praying, Judy, no matter how hard it is to do. It is *the one thing you can do*. Pray for the surgeon's hands, knowledge, and abilities. Pray that God might see fit to take this cup from you . . . that you might glorify him and lead your family through what lies ahead. Gather yourself and let God be your strength. . . ."

Girded by their love I began to pray, telling myself, *Gather yourself and let God be your strength*. As I prayed, the gaping hole in my heart began to fill with the hope I needed to face the challenges in the days ahead.

Today, just six weeks later, Ryan was given a clean bill of health from doctors at All Children's. No cancer was found in his blood, liver, or the mass surgeons removed from his chest. So tonight, as I laid my head to rest, I whispered a prayer of thanks for Henry and Marcy, our internet intercessors who gathered me in when I was weak—showing me how to let God be my strength.

Friends are those people who "storm the heavens" for

us, passionately placing our petitions on the throne of

God when we are too weak to cry out for help.

Acknowledgments

*W*e would like to dedicate this book to all of our friends—old, new, and those we've yet to meet. We've had the honor of writing about many of you and would not have the stories we've shared from our hearts without you.

Most of all, we would like to thank our friend and editor, Sharon Robie. Sharon, without your vision for the *God Things Come in Small Packages* series and your wholehearted trust in us, we might have missed a precious "God Thing" in our lives. What a blessing it has been working with you, Dave, and the entire team at Starburst Publishers. You have gained our utmost respect, and your enthusiasm has kept us seeking God's best for the inspiration needed to touch lives with our words.

We thank God for you and all that you have deposited into our lives as writers. As our friend you have reflected a ray of God to us.

We Love You!

Susan, Judy, and LeAnn

God Things Come in Small Packages for Friends: Exploring the Freedom of Friendship

LeAnn Weiss, Susan Duke, and Judy Carden

A heartwarming combination of true stories, paraphrased Scripture, and reflections that celebrate the simple yet cherished blessings shared between true friends. A new release from the elegant *God Things Come in Small Packages* series that combines the beauty of gift books with the depth of devotionals. Includes reflective meditation, narrative vignettes detailing powerful moments of revelation, and encouraging Scripture passages presented as letters to a friend.
(hard cover) ISBN 1892016346 $12.95

God Things Come in Small Packages for Women: Celebrating the Unique Gifts of Women

LeAnn Weiss, Susan Duke, and Judy Carden

Women will experience God's love like never before through powerfully translated Scripture, true stories, and reflections that celebrate the unique character of women. A new release from the elegant *God Things Come in Small Packages* series that combines the beauty of gift books with the depth of devotionals. Includes reflective meditation, narrative vignettes detailing powerful moments of revelation, and encouraging Scripture passages presented as letters from God.
(hard cover) ISBN 1892016354 $12.95

God Things Come in Small Packages for Moms: Rejoicing in the Simple Pleasures of Motherhood

Susan Duke, LeAnn Weiss, Caron Loveless, and Judy Carden

The "small" treasures God plants in a mom's day shine in this delightful book. Savor priceless stories, which encourage you to value treasures like a shapeless, ceramic bowl presented with a toothy grin; a child's hand clinging to yours on a crowded bus; or a handful of wildflowers presented on a hectic day. Each story combines personalized Scripture with heartwarming vignettes and inspiring reflections.
(hard cover) ISBN 189201629X $12.95

God Things Come in Small Packages: Celebrating the Little Things in Life
Susan Duke, LeAnn Weiss, Caron Loveless, and Judy Carden
Enjoy touching reminders of God's simple yet generous gifts to brighten our
days and gladden our hearts! Treasures like a sunset over a vast, sparkling ocean;
a child's trust; or the crystalline dew on a spider's web come to life in this elegant
compilation. Such occasions should be celebrated as if gift wrapped from God;
they're his hallmarks! Personalized Scripture is artfully combined with com-
pelling stories and reflections.
(hard cover) ISBN 1892016281 $12.95

Purchasing Information

www.starburstpublishers.com

Books are available from your favorite bookstore, either from current stock or
special order: use title, author, and ISBN. If unable to purchase from a bookstore, you may order direct from STARBURST PUBLISHERS. When ordering
please enclose full payment plus shipping and handling as follows:

Post Office (4th class)
$3.00 with purchase of up to $20.00
$4.00 ($20.01–$50.00)
5% of purchase price for purchases of $50.01 and up

Canada
$5.00 (up to $35.00)
15% ($35.01 and up)

United Parcel Service (UPS)
$4.50 (up to $20.00)
$6.00 ($20.01–$50.00)
7 % ($50.01 and up)

Overseas
$5.00 (up to $25.00)
20% ($25.01 and up)

Payment in U.S. funds only. Please allow two to four weeks minimum for delivery by USPS
(longer for overseas and Canada). Allow two to seven working days for delivery by UPS. Make
checks payable to and mail to: Starburst Publishers®, P.O. Box 4123, Lancaster, PA 17604.
Credit card orders may be placed by calling 1-800-441-1456, Mon–Fri, 8:30 A.M. to 5:30 P.M.
Eastern Standard Time. Prices are subject to change without notice. Catalogs are available for
a 9 x 12 self-addressed envelope with four first-class stamps.